wearing green.

Elijah Fern

BookLeaf
Publishing

India | USA | UK

Presentation by *BookLeaf Publishing*

Web: www.bookleafpub.com

E-mail: info@bookleafpub.com

ISBN: 9789357444736

First edition 2022

DEDICATION

dedicated to all the beautiful people who feel trapped, scared, and voiceless.

PREFACE

Hi, my name is Elijah Fern and I'm far too
young to be telling you how to live your life.
Within these pages I hope to share with you a
story that hits rather close to home, the story of
how a boy with dreams grew up to be a slightly
older boy with too many dreams.
you can start from the beginning if you like, or
maybe read back to front. it's up to you.

children.

When you look at a child you see carelessness.
But it's okay, they just don't know,
But they will learn soon enough!
They have a very long time to go.
When they're young they don't remember,
all the things that you will say.
But that's not true, none of it is.
It never really goes away.

performing.

Music.
Loud music blaring through the wooden walls of
our home.
Happy dances and colorful wonder,
but I only dance cause I'm drowning under
The pressure.
The pressure of a legacy.
Performing.
Performing cause I said I'd be
an asset to the family.
A family of happy smiles,
blinding lights and crowds going wild.
Point your toes, strike a pose,
Tuck in your stomach, tie a bow.
You have time to cry tonight when you sit at the
window and watch the solitary street light,
Blinking in peaceful loneliness.
Bitter sweet ignorance.
Tomorrow you'll put on your velcro shoes,
Head into school and put on your show.
But tonight you don't have to choose,
which creative path to follow.
Deep breath, little boy.
It will only go down hill tomorrow.

color.

Everything has color in my mind,
Foods, smells, faces, textures.
The sound of someone's voice, harsh or kind,
ignites my brain with RGB and HEX codes.
I look out across the garden at dusk,
And see an insect on a leaf.
Its shell a mix of metallic hues, it's husk
the color of an oil leak.
At night when you arrive at your favorite
restaurant,
The sound of laughter and the smell of pasta
Swirls through the atmosphere, and after,
You collapse into bed and let yourself sink.
Your thoughts wander and you let yourself think.
These feelings, a sunset;
Stabs of autumnal colors.
Then the paint drips away,
And the colors are replaced by others.
At the beach on a bleak day,
It starts to pour; the shore
Mixes with the sky on a palette of emotion.
Cadmium, cerulean, pthalo, ocean.
Even at my young age,
My brain has a full rainbow of memories.
Every moment, every person.

All the individual stories.

god.

Was I alone that night?
HELLO? a sound so frightful
it shakes the trees with omnipotent might.
Does he stand here in the garden
with nothing but an empty universe around him,
This little boy?
What if he falls and breaks his bones,
And his china toy, all on his own.
Who will call out HELLO? then?
A face appears out of the stars,
A woman with pointed ears and glowing eyes,
Her touch is soft, though her skin has scars.
She picks me up, into heavenly skies.
Is this the God I've read about,
Are the books too long for me to understand?
She looks different here.
I bury my face into her hand.
I no longer fear falling, though I am so high.
I trust God's guidance through the starlit sky.
Though as I drift into sleep, I feel myself slip,
And I plummet through space and out of sight.
No one catches me when I land.
Now I understand
Why are the books so long?
The writer fears the end.

boys.

I kissed a boy in second grade,
His face against mine as he stared into my eyes.
He pulled back smiling, I guess it made
He laughed, though it gave me butterflies.
We were ridiculed and punished for our
misguided actions,
Our tutors swear that we sin against God.
But I know if God doesn't mind if I fall to my
death,
She doesn't stop the names; "queer" and "odd",
Who do I trust?
She abandoned me at my worst,
Left me alone in the dust.
Throwing me out of the sky.
I could rebel against society and not comply,
But why?
Why should I expose myself to the hate I'd get,
Just to follow the voice inside my head.
Remember to point your toes, strike a pose.
Smile through the pain, and you won't gain
Happiness.
But you'll seem sane.
And maybe that is all I want,
As selfish as it may be, God!

I am in control of my actions,
So I'll divide myself into uneven factions.
Parts of me I'll hide forever,
Some I will display to the world.
I'll continue to dance and sing, but never
Tell them that you like both boys and girls.
Never tell them, Eli.
Never.

stories.

My parents were divorced when I was five.
I moved away from my home,
into an alien life.
I struggled at school,
had no friends, at the end
I didn't feel like I had accomplished anything.
The movies that I watched,
All the books that I read,
The characters in them always ended up dead.
And the people always cared,
Always miss them when they're gone.
And I wished for something bad,
Something different, something wrong.
Cause until I was dead,
No one really cared.
I lived an interesting life,
Full of pain and hurt.
But the people in the movies,
They always had it worse.
And I longed for that,
longed that my life would be worthy
Of a poster for a book tour,
Or the premier
of a movie.

So I wrote myself stories that weren't really
there,
Filled in what was missing, made myself care.
I lived in my head, no limits or boundaries.
Running through fantasies, feet and heart
pounding
I spent hours here, until two worlds started to
merge.
I couldn't differentiate my imagination from the
real world.
I was always too worried my ship would start to
sink,
So instead of seizing the day, I would just think
and think.

rain.

When it rains, the streets go dark.
The shiny pavement, or a puddle in a park
reflects a whole other world, exciting and new.
A world without touch, nerves, feelings too.
A world without touch is a world without pain.
The water on the window of an electric train,
as you head into the city, street lights shimmer.
The sunlight fades as the world gets dimmer.
Water streams down your cheeks, and floods
your eyes,
you squint as you gaze into the hazy skies.
And no matter if you scream, dance, shout or
cry.
Nobody will care to look, even if you try.
That's what's beautiful about it.
You're actually alone.
You take a small moment to glance up from your
phone,
and you might really see that water falling from
space,
as simplistic as it is, it rinses your face
and you can finally see.
You can see yourself.
In store front window at eleven at night,

You're granted true sight, as you gaze into the bright
eyes of the child inside you.
The ones you know best.
And yet they confuse you.
Why do they confuse you?
Because you're not used to caring.
Caring about small things,
while sharing a smile with your reflection.
Pay attention.

ferns.

What's in a name? Does it define you?
Is the word your friends will call
describe what's inside you?
If you're named from your father,
Does it mean that you're leaving?
If your named from your grandma,
Does it mean you'll stop breathing?
When you're walking in a forest,
in a sea of spiraling green,
you don't notice the ferns
blending in with the scene.
And though my father leaves,
And grandma doesn't breathe,
The most subtle of leaves in the evening eaves,
of the rainforest trees, ferns hide underneath.
At a glance, they're not much,
but the life that resides with them!
Beatles and bugs,
I just wish I could hide with them.
Not as tall as the rest,
on the dark forest floor.
They don't invoke intrigue or awe,
but i'm sure
if you took just a moment.

Then you will find,
that the bushes of ferns are really quite kind.
Yet I'm stuck on a pedestal, all glittered up.
Waiting to be gawked at like the biggest of trees,
I'm not like a fern hiding deep in the leaves.
How I wish I could go a day without being me.
Escape from the canopy.

dreams.

Sometimes I forget where I go when I'm
sleeping.
It feels like I am flying, or more likely falling.
It feels like I'm riding a boat down the rapids,
on the back of a dragon, weaving through clouds
up and
over the rainbow. everything I'm able
to think of can happen.
But then reality hits me, gives me a slap in
the face.
I'm awake.
And this entire time, I was lying in bed.
These mighty adventures were all in my head.
I pack my bag and head off to school,
ready to face the onslaught of ridicule.
People say, "Follow your dreams, grab the pen!"
But if my dreams aren't real, how do I follow
them?

bread.

I can't eat bread.
If I eat it, it messes with my head,
I won't wind up dead, but like I said,
I can't eat it.
When going to a party, or a friends house
maybe,
I'll try not to eat bread, but sometimes they
make me.
Cause the thing is, it's not bread that'll mess
with me.
It's gluten! A substance in almost everything.
So sweets, ice cream, chocolate and cake,
muffins, donuts, anything baked.
I don't want to say no to the things that they give
me,
but you never really know what it's in, so
forgive me.
I'm no fun at parties, really. But I'm just being
cautious.
But you know when we let something consume
all of us.
A characteristic, or a thing that we do.
We get known just for that, no matter what we
do.
Last day of school, they corner me on the grass.

"You're not going anywhere unless you swear for us."
Not once had I sworn here, so I just said, "No."
But they wouldn't let me go unless I gave them a show.
I let this thing consume me, as I stood in it's shadow.
But I ran from the group, made it safely to the meadow.
Don't you fucking do it, I was saying in my head.
So I'll never eat bread.
Just in case.

food.

Growing up as a dancer,
you don't get to choose,
how you look, how you eat,
the way you wear your shoes.
It's always a contest,
with your friends and your peers.
Comparing yourself to others,
bringing yourself to tears.
Going into school,
with a lunch box packed.
But you throw away your food,
maybe eat a few snacks.
Everyone you see,
looks better than you.
Not just the hot ones,
but the ugly ones too.
Every single comment counts.
I can't state that enough.
Someone says I have skinny arms,
and now I pray to be buff,
it's not enough.
All the stuff that you yell,
light hearted fun,
takes a blow to my soul,
It makes my mind run.

I look in the mirror.
Stop and stare.
I get straight A's, I am successful.
Why should I care?

green.

Why do we have favorite things?
For the excitement that it brings,
For our own identities,
so someone looks at me and sees
the kind of person that I am.
Your favorite song by your favorite band.
Your favorite view and your favorite smell,
Favorite name, book, and color as well.
Favorite color… there's so many i've seen.
But I think I'd have to settle on green.
In the natural world, you don't notice it.
It's everywhere, but no one picks it.
Camouflage is shades of green,
and all the pretty places i've been
are green.
So I wear it. Wear green on my skin.
It hides the things I hide within.
Wearing green, a painted face.
A mask to cover the disgrace
that I see when I look at me.
One, two and three,
Count the insecurities.
Forty nine, fifty.
If he changes, IF he
became someone he wants to be.

Then maybe.

Maybe he could wear pink?

performing (pt2).

When I was in grade five or so,
I was put on the front of a newspaper article.
My teacher pulled it up in front of the class,
Told them to say good job,
Have a toast, raise a glass.
Though they just rolled their eyes and whined,
Called me a show off for showing off my fine
wine.
But that it is okay,
I don't do it for them anyway.
I don't do it for those primary school classes.
I don't perform for the numbers or the masses.
Getting to stand on a stage,
And get paid a minimum wage,
To pretend you are someone else?
It's a blessing, and it helps.
It helped me overcome anxiety,
Talking for thousands of watching eyes.
It helped me be confident in my identity,
Be who I am and stop telling lies.
I gotta be so many people,
With their terrible problems,
but none of them were mine.
I would leave the theater and be fine.
And yet it was still selfish of me,

For escaping.

sleep.

Life is hard, that's not a secret.
But not when it's night time. No, not all of it.
Every single day we are living in a life,
That was created for us by the ones before our
time.
We didn't choose to be here,
Not today, not in a year,
No.
I spend my day doing things for adults,
So when it's night, I do things for myself.
Though I'm afraid to turn the light out,
I'm terrified to go to sleep.
Because I know that once I wake up,
I will get up, hold my head up,
Talk my friends up, pull my grades up.
And afterwards I'm fed up.
And the less that I sleep, the longer I'll have,
To dread the inevitable dreadful drag,
And sit in my room without following orders.
Lying on the floor and staring at my posters.
My fan slowly spins, as does my mind.
And if I sit there long enough I'll find
That it's not the morning that I fear.
It's sleep, and it's almost here.
I don't cry, though I am scared.

I almost wished that I cared,
But I don't because I'm used to it.
This is just life.
This is it.

older.

When you're a kid, everything is a count down.
When will my next birthday be?
Or Christmas, or the next time i'll see
my grandparents. Years will seem so long.
And I know there is like a million songs
About growing up, and getting older.
But none of them explain how much colder
you feel when you're old, only sixteen.
And now I have seen just how selfish I've been.
Now my grandparents are gone,
and so is the excitement Christmas brings.
It's just another year, another day.
Even if the sleigh bell rings.
We use to laugh as the new year came,
as we adjusted our brain to remember the date.
Twenty-twelve, thirteen, sixteen, twenty.
Through the years i have left are really quite
plenty,
I constantly feel like my times running short,
Who would've thought.
And have I ought to remind you,
That as days pass, you don't leave it all behind
you.
The weight of it all piles up in a heap

Makes me weep, as I sleep in this miserable
heap,
of pillows and blankets, not special or
memorable.
One day I'll just die, disappointing and
forgettable.

love.

This is a topic that I've been avoiding.
Because it's not easy to record.
We crave it as humans, though it is scary.
You flirt, and you date, and you kiss, and you marry.
And then there's your life laid out on a plate.
Date after date, and now it's your fate.
Do I still love though I fear their loss?
What is the point? What is the cost?
I've blocked out all of these feelings before.
So I'll do it again, but this time more.
This time I'll block out my self love too.
And block the love from family, who
says that they will love me forever.
I said that too.
I wasn't as clever then.
But now, oh now, it won't ever show.
Trust me, 1 know that feelings only grow.
But sometimes you just have to let it go…

girls.

A boy.
A girl.
Two souls with wanderlust,
Wanting someone more than just
A friend who doesn't really care.
Too focused on their perfect hair.
You've seen the way he looks at her,
A fleeting glance, a symphonic blur.
No they aren't friends, they rarely speak,
She notices him like once a week.
They greet each other as they pass
On their way to science class.
It's a love story with a written end.
Planned and perfect as it stands.
It's hardly love, as you'll find,
He's not in love, he doesn't mind.

silence.

Every day is filled with noise.
The shrieking shouts of girls and boys.
You barely get a moment's rest,
It's a constant swirling sound. Unless,
Occasionally there's a single second,
A time that you can take a breath and
It only happens very rarely.
I can only remember them barely,
But I'll never forget these blissful times.
They're never going to leave my mind.
Even if there's noise around,
Your brain just blocks off all the sound.
As you gaze into the eyes of a lover,
Or you walk alone in a rainy shower.
Visiting a hiding place,
From when you were nearly eight.
A windy day on a lonely beach,
Each and every plum or peach.
Sunrises and sunsets, and
The very first time you held someone's hand.
That moment when you realize,
At night in the city with sparkling skies,
That every person has their very own lives.
You are small, insignificant in size.
And yet you are just so important.

acceptance.

The rarest thing to find, by far,
Is someone who is at peace with who they are.
I still have a long way to go.
You never know, maybe tomorrow.
I once said it all goes down hill.
Maybe it will.
Or maybe I'll wake
with a smile on my face,
and yell at the sky,
"I NO LONGER FEAR FALLING THOUGH I
AM SO HIGH.

www.ingramcontent.com/pod-product-compliance
Lightning Source LLC
Chambersburg PA
CBHW050751180726
48003CB00020B/2339